THE HEART

of an

INTERCESSOR

PROPHETIC PRAYER JOURNAL

*"Let us draw near with a true heart in full assurance of
faith, having our hearts sprinkled from an evil
conscience, and our bodies washed with pure water"
(Hebrews 10:22).*

JENILLE DANIELS

Foreword by Sarah Morgan

The Heart of an Intercessor: Prophetic
Prayer Journal
Copyright © 2020 by Jenille Daniels.

Author's Contact Information
Email – designsbycreativityllc@gmail.com
Instagram – designsbycreativityllc

Published by Morgan Publishing
3701 Inglewood, CA 90278 Redondo
Beach, CA
1-888-320-5622 Ext. 1

ISBN: 978-1-5136-6203-9

.

DEDICATION

This book is dedicated:

To the God of my destiny, Jesus Christ, my personal Lord and Savior, and the precious Holy Spirit, my Senior Partner and Helper. Thank you for being with me forever.

I am eternally grateful for the strong support of my sweet and amazing husband, Leiran Daniels. You have walked with me and, at times, held me as I journeyed through this process. I Love you forever.

To our three beautiful children Malik, Malia, and London. You are miracles from God, the Father. You sacrificed and took on additional responsibilities to support me in the completion of this assignment. Boldly walk in your purpose and fulfill your destiny!

To my loving mother, Norma Jane Castillo, who has prayed and ministered to me since the day she discovered I was in her womb. May your head never lack oil.

To my beautiful sisters, Sharol Maximo and Dorian Castillo, and my brother, Earl Castillo, I Love and appreciate you dearly.
To my niece and nephew, Makada and Jahmari, be all that God has called you to be!

To my loving family, who has been an incredible support to me, words cannot express how much I appreciate you.

TABLE OF CONTENTS

FOREWORD

I am humbled yet elated as I pen this forward for one whom I can unequivocally say that she not only wears the mantle but has over the years developed the heart of an Intercessor, Jenille Daniels.

David, who shared the same lineage as Jesus, functioned as a King, a Prophet, and a Priest; hence was a great intercessor, one who stood before God first and then stood between Him and His People as a mediator. As an intercessor, he understood that more than his words, that the posture of his heart would cause God's ears to incline to his prayers. Many of his prayers, as he pursued the presence and audience of His King, were directed in that area. As a result, he was known as a man after God's heart.

"Search me, God, and know my heart; test me and know my concerns,"

"Look deep into my heart, God, and find out everything I am thinking" (CEV).

"Examine me, O God, and know my mind; test me, and discover my thoughts" (Psalms 139:23-24 - GNT).

David presented his heart and gave God permission to search it, cleanse it, and even recreate it so that his prayers would never be hindered.

> *"If I regard iniquity in my heart, the Lord will not hear me"* (Psalms 66:18).

> *"The heart is deceitful above all things, and desperately wicked: who can know it? I the Lord search the heart, I try the reins, even to give every man according to his ways, and according to the fruit of his doings"* (Jeremiah 17: 9).

> *"Blessed are the pure in heart: for they shall see God"* (Matthew 5:8).

The heart is not just a muscle that pumps blood. It is said that you cannot understand a human being until you know their heart. That is why man looks at the outward appearance, but God looks at the heart. The Bible describes the heart as your inner man [spirit, soul, mind, emotions, passions, will, etc.]. The heart is the real you, where your beliefs affect your behavior. It is the control center of your life. Why do I do the things I do? Why am I so angry? Why is my life so depressed? Why was my family awesome one day, but now it seems like guerrilla warfare? Why do I get angry in traffic? Why is she so critical and controlling? Why is he so ungrateful? Why is she so afraid? Why won't he talk? Why am I the way I am? The simple answer is the heart. There is something seriously wrong with your heart. Your control center has a glitch in the mainframe.

What is the matter with the heart? It is stained with sin. Sin is like the fat that clogs your heart from functioning properly. *Whatever rules your heart will exercise inescapable influence over your life and behavior.* Whatever you treasure will control your heart, "where your treasure is, your heart will be also" (Matthew 6:21). Whatever controls your heart will control your behavior, "no one can serve two masters" (Matthew 6:24).

It is impossible to know the heart of another man because you can only see the outside of a man [behavior]. However, Hebrews 4:12-13 tells you that the Bible is like a scalpel. It cuts through layers of flesh and exposes the condition of your heart. Although you do not have x-ray vision to any man's heart, God and His Word do. The Word of God is a heart-revealer. The Word of God has the power to change your heart. That is, the Bible compares itself to a surgical tool that can cut to the innermost part of your soul—the heart. For without a heart change, there is no real change. The heart is your control center. Your heart thinks, remembers, feels, desires, craves, experiences, decides, and acts. In other words, your heart is the base of operation for your cognition, affection, and volition. What your heart believes will affect your attitude, behavior, and actions. Relationships, society, and culture might influence your heart, but they are not the cause of your heart's control. You are in control of your internal responses to what is happening externally. What should your response be to sinful external influences?

> *"With confidence draw near to the throne of grace, that*
> *you may receive mercy and find grace to help in the time*
> *of need"* (Hebrews 4:14-16)

In *The Heart of an Intercessor*, Jenille, as an Intercessor chosen from the furnace of affliction, and one whose heart has been circumcised by the cutting away of the foreskin of sin and the world by the Word of God skillfully allures us to the secret of the success of every true spirit-filled intercessor; that is to allow God to examine and investigate our hearts, purify our hearts, and re-orient the posture so that God will not only hear but also answer our prayers. In this journal, Jenille challenges you as an Intercessor to ask some great x-ray questions to see the condition of your heart, preparing you for potential heart change, that positions you for answered prayer.

I encourage you through this journal to prayerfully and sincerely ask yourself tough heart questions as if you are getting a thorough examination from the heart doctor. You would not want to be careless because your condition could be as severe as an impending heart attack. When you ask questions of the heart, do not rebuttal. Willingly accept the facts as they are and use them to motivate you towards change. God the Father has given you Christ whom, if allowed, will do surgery on your heart, opening up the clogged arteries and capillaries so His life-giving power can cleanse you from the consequences of a sinful heart. If you have never opened up the door to your heart to God, today is the day. He holds the keys to the kingdom. He is the door to new life.

Only He can give you a new heart that is fully satisfied in Him. Make Christ the passion of your heart as He gives you "The Heart of an Intercessor."

Jenille, I commend you on a job well done, that as the Lord continues to search for an Intercessor in the earth, because of this Journal, He will never have to wonder!

> *"He saw that there was no man, And **wondered** that there was no intercessor"* (Isaiah 59:16).

Sarah Morgan

Prayer Academy, Los Angeles, California.

ACKNOWLEDGMENTS

To my spiritual leaders, Bishop Deon Douglas, and his lovely wife, Prophetess Fannette Douglas. Thank you for your prayers, labor of love, and words of encouragement!

To Dr. Sarah Morgan, thank you for believing in me, praying for me, standing with me, teaching, and demonstrating that anything not birthed through Prayer is illegal!

To Bishop William Peter Morgan, thank you for helping me to identify and walk in my calling and purpose through the counsel of God's Word.

To Pastor Rochelle Hess, I am forever grateful for every spiritual investment that you have imparted into my life and all the prayers that you have made on my behalf. I Love you!

To every Intercessor across the globe, may your Prayers of Intercession continue to touch the heart of God. May your prayers bring change, transform lives, turn hearts back to God, heal souls, set lives free, and reconcile and restore marriages to the original example of Christ, as the Bridegroom, and us as the bride.

To Prophetess Karla Allen, thank you for your commitment, dedication, words of encouragement, and being my destiny helper for this masterpiece in excellence!

INTRODUCTION

A ccording to scripture, Jesus is the Chief Intercessor, who is seated at the right hand of God, making intercession for you and me.

"So then, after the Lord had spoken to them, He was received up into heaven, and sat down at the right hand of God" (**Mark 16:19**).

"Likewise, the Spirit also helps in our weaknesses. For we do not know what we should pray for as we ought, but the Spirit Himself makes intercession for us with groanings which cannot be uttered" (**Romans 8:26**).

"Now He who searches the hearts knows what the mind of the Spirit is, because He makes intercession for the saints according to the will of God" (**Romans 8:27**).

"Who is he who condemns? It is Christ who died, and furthermore is also risen, who is even at the right hand of God, who also makes intercession for us" (**Romans 8:34**).

As you present your prayer request before Jehovah God, in Jesus' Name, the Holy Spirit will make intercession for you. You will receive the grace necessary to pray prophetically by the Spirit of revelation, as you press into God's presence to hear His Voice.

> *"If My people who are called by My name will humble themselves, and pray and seek My face, and turn from their wicked ways, then I will hear from heaven, and will forgive their sin and heal their land"* (**2 Chronicles 7:14**).

> *"The Lord has heard my supplication; The Lord will receive my prayer"* (**Psalm 6:9**).

INTERCESSOR DEFINED

An intercessor is one who stands before God on behalf of others. An intercessor links God's mercy with human need. An intercessor makes intercession to the Lord. An intercessor assists **in the birthing of the movements of God in the earth realm.**

An Intercessor is one who **paga's** which is to reach; to meet someone; to pressure or urge someone strongly; to meet up with a person; encounter, entreat; to assail with urgent petitions. Intercession involves reaching God, meeting God, and entreating Him for His favor.

An intercessor is one who has a heart's cry for God's people and His nation. An intercessor is willing to rend his or her heart and stand in the gap. An intercessor is willing to make committed intercession between God and man to repair breaches and mend what is broken.

An intercessor's heart cannot be overtaken with:

Unforgiveness	Malice	Evil
Offense	Rebellion	Deceit
Bitterness	Envy	Lies
Resentment	Jealousy	Perversion
Anger	Disobedience	Deception

Pride	Lust	Greed
Wickedness	Iniquity	Self-centered
ambitions		

Rather, our hearts must be:

Loyal	Firm	Unwavering
Resolute	Faithful	Committed
Dedicated	Dependable	Reliable
Steady	True	Constant
Staunch	Solid	Trusty
Uncompromising	Unyielding	Unhesitating
Unfaltering	Relentless	Single-minded

> *"My heart is steadfast, O God, my heart is steadfast; I will sing and give praise" (Psalm 57:7).*

The fruit of the Spirit must be evident in the life of an intercessor.

> *"But the fruit of the Spirit is love, joy, peace, longsuffering, kindness, goodness, faithfulness, gentleness, self-control. Against such there is no law" (Galatians 5:22-23).*

An intercessor maintains a steadfast heart flowing with the fruit of the Spirit by abiding in Christ. An intercessor whose heart is right before God will see desire fulfilled.

"If you abide in Me, and My words abide in you, you will ask what you desire, and it shall be done for you" (**John 15:7**).

WHAT HINDERS THE PRAYERS OF AN INTERCESSOR?

In order for us to walk in the agape love of God through His Son, Jesus Christ, we must walk in true heartfelt forgiveness. Lack of forgiveness blocks access to the Kingdom of God and His marvelous power.

"By this we know love, because He laid down His life for us. And we also ought to lay down our lives for the brethren. But whoever has this world's goods and sees his brother in need, and shuts up his heart from him, how does the love of God abide in him? My little children let us not love in word or in tongue, but indeed and in truth. And by this we know that we are of the truth and shall assure our hearts before Him. For if our heart condemns us, God is greater than our heart and knows all things. Beloved, if our heart does not condemn us, we have confidence toward God. And whatever we ask we receive from Him, because we keep His commandments and do those things that are pleasing in His sight. And this is His commandment: that we should believe on the name of His Son Jesus Christ and love one another, as He gave us commandment" (**1 John 3:16-23**).

"For You, Lord, are good, and ready to forgive, And abundant in mercy to all those who call upon You" ***(Psalm 86:5).***

Goodness and forgiveness are attributes birthed by our heavenly Father and expected to be found active in the heart of the intercessor. God does not want us to portion out mercy and forgiveness with teaspoons. He is looking for people who distribute forgiveness and mercy with huge shovels.

"So Jesus answered and said to them "Have faith in God. For assuredly, I say to you, whoever says to this mountain, Be removed and cast into the sea, and does not doubt in His heart, but believes that those things he says will be done, he will have whatever he says. Therefore I say to you, whatever things you ask when you pray, believe that you receive them, and you will have them. And whenever you stand praying if you have anything against anyone forgive him, that your Father in heaven may also forgive you your trespasses. But if you do not forgive, neither will your Father in heaven forgive your trespasses" ***(Mark 11:22-26).***

JOURNALING YOUR WAY TO VICTORY

*"Let the words of my mouth and the meditation of my heart Be acceptable in Your sight O Lord my strength and my Redeemer" (**Psalm 19:14**).*

Journal Strategy

Read and meditate on the provided scriptures. After you have meditated on the scripture, you will journal about whatever you believe God is speaking to your heart.

*"Be anxious for nothing, but in everything by prayer and supplication, with thanksgiving let your request be made known to God; and the peace of God, which surpasses all understanding, will guard your hearts and minds through Christ Jesus" (**Philippians 4:6-7**).*

Prayer Request

Ask Holy Spirit for what or whom does God want you to pray? What does He desire to do for you, a loved one, a friend, your city, or your nation? Write those requests, so that you can chronicle the goodness and faithfulness of God over time.

"But if they are prophets, and if the Word of the Lord is with them now make intercession to the Lord of hosts" (Jeremiah 27:18).

Prophetic Prayer

Prophetic prayer is prayer initiated within the heart of the intercessors by Holy Spirit. Always remember that Holy Spirit is our Helper and our Teacher.

In the place of prophetic prayer, Holy Spirit will reveal to you what to pray according to the Heart and the mind of the Father.

"Call to Me, and I will answer you, and show you Great and mighty things, you do not know" (Jeremiah 33:3).

What is God Saying to YOU?

We pray and make intercession in faith, trusting God's Word and promises to come into manifestation. Write down whatever God reveals to you.

DECLARATIONS

Day by Day as you take your spiritual walk with God through this Prayer Journal make these declarations over your life:

1. I prophetically declare and believe in faith that you are healed mentally, emotionally, physically, psychologically, spiritually, and financially.

2. I make a prophetic declaration over your life that you are prospering spiritually, emotionally, physically, and financially, in Jesus' Mighty Name!

3. I prophetically declare that your mind, body, and soul are healed through the shed BLOOD of Jesus Christ, our Lord, and Savior.

4. I prophetically declare that you are refreshed, revived, renewed and restored, in Jesus' Name.

5. I prophetically declare you will birth greatness through these lines and pages, in Jesus' Name.

6. I prophetically declare you are walking in your God-given purpose and destiny in the joy of the Lord, in Jesus' Name.

7. I prophetically declare that you will receive the revelation of your assignment and that His Kingdom will be glorified through you in the earth realm, in Jesus' Name.

8. My prayer for you is that you will walk this out in courage and boldness in Jesus' Mighty Name!

"Be Strong and of good courage, do not fear nor be afraid of them; for the Lord your God, He is the One who goes with you. He will not leave you nor forsake you" (**Deuteronomy 31:6**).

"The Lord will perfect that which concerns me; Your mercy, O Lord, endures forever; Do not forsake the works of your hands" (**Psalm 138:8**).

"When we pray in secret, God rewards us in the open" (**Matthew 6:6**).

"Jesus said to him I am the way the truth, and the life. No one comes to the Father except through Me" (**John 14:6**).

"But may the God of all grace who called you to his eternal glory by Christ Jesus, after you have suffered a while, perfect, establish, strengthen, and settle

you. To Him be the glory and the dominion forever and ever. Amen" (*1 Peter 5:10-11*).

"For we wrestle not against flesh and blood, but against principalities, against powers, against the rulers of the darkness of this world, against spiritual wickedness in high places. Wherefore take unto you the whole armor of God, that ye may be able to withstand in the evil day and having done all to stand. Stand therefore, having your loins girt about with truth and having on the breastplate of righteousness; And your feet shod with the preparation of the gospel of peace; Above all taking the shield of faith, wherewith ye shall be able to quench all the fiery darts of the wicked. And take the helmet of salvation, and the sword of the spirit, which is the Word Of God. Praying always with all prayer and supplication in the Spirit, and watching thereunto with all perseverance and supplication for all saints" (*Ephesians 6:12-18*).

"For the weapons of our warfare are not carnal but mighty in God for pulling down of strongholds, casting down arguments and every high thing that *exalts itself against the knowledge of God, bringing every thought into captivity to the obedience of Christ, and being ready to punish all disobedience when obedience is fulfilled"* **(2 Corinthians 10:4-6).**

This Prayer Journal Belongs to:

_____

SCRIPTURE FOR MEDITATION AND MEMORIZATION

The Eternity of God and Man's Frailty

*"So teach us to number our days, That we may gain a heart of Wisdom. Return, O Lord How long? And have compassion on Your servants. Oh, satisfy us early with your mercy, That we may rejoice and be glad all our days! Make us glad according to the days in which You have afflicted us, The years in which we have seen evil. Let your work appear to your servants, And Your glory to their children. And let the beauty of the Lord our God be upon us, And establish the works of our hands for us; Yes, establish the work of our hands" (**Psalm 90:12-17**).*

Prayers for Mercy, with Meditation on the Excellencies of the Lord.

*"Teach me Your way, O Lord; I will walk in Your truth; Unite my heart to fear your name" (**Psalm 86:11**).*

"The heart is deceitful above all things, And desperately wicked who can know it? I, the Lord, search the heart I test the mind, Even to give every man according to his ways, According to the fruit of His doings" **(Jeremiah 17:9).**

The Heart is the inner-self, which thinks, feels, and acts.

"Keep your heart with all diligence, For out of it spring the issues of life" **(Proverbs 4:23).**

"But what does it say? The word is near you, in your mouth and in your heart" (that is, the word of faith which we preach): that if you confess with your mouth the Lord Jesus and believe in your heart that God has raised Him from the dead, you will be saved. For with the heart one believes unto righteousness, and with the mouth confession is made unto salvation" **(Romans 10:8-10).**

The Heart

IT'S A MATTER OF THE HEART

There are times in our lives, and even in our walk with God when we want to give up, throw in the towel, throw out the rug, turn back and scream, "just forget it!" When we find ourselves in these moments, we can be encouraged to know what is declared in the Word of God.

"And let us not grow weary while doing good, for in due season we shall reap if we do not lose heart" (**Galatians 6:9**).

I prophesy that you will see the manifestation of your due season. You will see the due season for your marriage, business, children, ministry, finances, relationships, your community, region, city, and nation.

I decree and declare, by faith, you will not miss your due season, but that you will reap it in its complete fullness, in the Mighty Name of Jesus Christ, the Son of the living God.

"I will praise You, O Lord my God, with all my heart, And I will glorify Your name forever. For great is Your mercy toward me, And you have delivered our soul from the depths of Sheol" (**Psalm 86: 12-13**).

Scripture Focus

Read, Meditate, Listen, Pray, Write

"And the Lord smelled a soothing aroma. Then the Lord said in His heart, I will never again curse the ground for man's sake, although the imagination of man's heart is evil from his youth; nor will I again destroy every living thing as I have done" **(Genesis 8:21).**

"For You, O Lord of hosts, God of Israel, have revealed this to Your servant, saying, 'I will build you a house.' Therefore Your servant has found it in his heart to pray this prayer to You" **(2 Samuel 7:27).**

_____

_____

_____

_____

_____

_____

_____

_____

_____

_____

_____

_____

Scripture Focus

Read, Meditate, Listen, Pray, Write

"But from there you will seek the Lord your God, and you will find Him if you seek Him with all your heart and with all your soul" (**Deuteronomy 4:29**).

"And the Lord said to him: I have heard your prayer and your supplication that you have made before Me; I have consecrated this house which you have built to put my name there forever, and My eyes and My heart will be there perpetually" (**1 Kings 9:3**).

_____

_____

_____

_____

_____

_____

_____

_____

_____

_____

_____

_____

_____

Scripture Focus

Read, Meditate, Listen, Pray, Write

*"You shall love the Lord your God with all your heart, with all your soul, and with all your strength" (**Deuteronomy 6:5**).*

*"Then Hezekiah prayed before the Lord, and said "O Lord God of Israel, the One who dwells between the cherubim, You are God, You alone, of all the kingdoms of the earth. You have made heaven and earth" (**2 Kings 19:15**).*

_____

_____

_____

_____

_____

_____

_____

_____

_____

_____

_____

_____

Scripture Focus

Read, Meditate, Listen, Pray, Write

*"And the Lord thy God will circumcise your heart and the heart of your descendants, to love the Lord your God with all your heart and with all your soul, that you may live" (**Deuteronomy 30:6**).*

*"Return and tell Hezekiah the leader of my people, 'Thus says the Lord, the God of David your father: "I have heard your prayer, I have seen your tears; surely I will heal you. On the third day you shall go up to the house of the Lord" (**2 Kings 20:5**).*

Scripture Focus

Read, Meditate, Listen, Pray, Write

"Now Hannah spoke in her heart; only her lips moved, but her voice was not heard. Therefore Eli thought she was drunk" (**1 Samuel 1:13**).

"Yet regard the prayer of Your servant and his supplication, O Lord my God, and listen to the cry and the prayer which Your servant is praying before you" (**2 Chronicles 6:19**).

_____

_____

_____

_____

_____

_____

_____

_____

_____

_____

_____

_____

_____

Scripture Focus

Read, Meditate, Listen, Pray, Write

"For You, O Lord of host, God of Israel, have revealed this to Your servant, saying, 'I will build you a house.' Therefore Your servant has found it in his heart to pray this prayer to You" (**2 Samuel 7:27**).

"That Your eyes may be open toward this temple day and night, toward the place where You said You would put Your name, that You may hear the prayer which Your servant makes toward this place" (**2 Chronicles 6:20**).

_____

_____

_____

_____

_____

_____

_____

_____

_____

_____

_____

_____

Scripture Focus

Read, Meditate, Listen, Pray, Write

"But the Lord said to Samuel, Do not look at his appearance or at his physical stature, because I have refused him. For the Lord does not see as man sees; for man looks at the outward appearance, but the Lord looks at the heart" (1 Samuel 16:7).

"Then hear from heaven their prayer and their supplication, and maintain their cause" (2 Chronicles 6:35).

_____

_____

_____

_____

_____

_____

_____

_____

_____

_____

_____

_____

Scripture Focus

Read, Meditate, Listen, Pray, Write

*"Let your heart therefore be loyal to the Lord our God, to walk in His statutes and keep His commandments, as at this day" (**1 Kings 8:61**).*

*"Then hear from heaven Your dwelling place their prayer and their supplications and maintain their cause, and forgive Your people who have sinned against You" (**2 Chronicles 6:39**).*

_____

_____

_____

_____

_____

_____

_____

_____

_____

_____

_____

_____

_____

_____

Scripture Focus

Read, Meditate, Listen, Pray, Write

*"But I have trusted in Your mercy; My heart shall rejoice in Your salvation "(**Psalm 13:5**).*

*"Now, my God, I pray let Your eyes be open and let Your ears be attentive to the prayer made in this place" (**2 Chronicles 6:40**).*

Scripture Focus

Read, Meditate, Listen, Pray, Write

"Let the words of my mouth and the meditation of my heart Be acceptable in Your sight, O Lord, my strength and my Redeemer" **(Psalm 19:14).**

"Then the Lord appeared to Solomon by night, and said to him: "I have heard your prayer, and have chosen this place for myself as a house of sacrifice" **(2 Chronicles 7:12).**

_____

_____

_____

_____

_____

_____

_____

_____

_____

_____

_____

_____

Scripture Focus

Read, Meditate, Listen, Pray, Write

"The poor shall eat and be satisfied; Those who seek Him will praise the Lord. Let your heart live forever!" (**Psalm 22:26**).

"Now my eyes will be open and My ears attentive to prayer made in this place" (**2 Chronicles 7:15**).

_____

_____

_____

_____

_____

_____

_____

_____

_____

_____

_____

_____

_____

Scripture Focus

Read, Meditate, Listen, Pray, Write

"Who may ascend into the hill of the Lord? Or who may stand in His holy place? He who has clean hands and a pure heart, Who has not lifted up his soul to an idol, Nor sworn deceitfully" (**Psalm 24:3-4**).

"Then the priest, the Levites, arose and blessed the people, and their voice was heard; and their prayer came up to His holy dwelling place to heaven" (**2 Chronicles 30:27**).

_____

_____

_____

_____

_____

_____

_____

_____

_____

_____

_____

_____

_____

Scripture Focus

Read, Meditate, Listen, Pray, Write

"Wait on the Lord; Be of good courage, And He shall strengthen your heart Wait I say on the Lord!" (**Psalm 27:14**).

"You will make your prayer to Him, He will hear you, And you will pay your vows" (**Job 22:27**).

_____

_____

_____

_____

_____

_____

_____

_____

_____

_____

_____

_____

_____

Scripture Focus

Read, Meditate, Listen, Pray, Write

"He who has clean hands and a pure heart, Who has not lifted up his soul to an idol, Nor sworn deceitfully. He shall receive blessing from the Lord" **(Psalm 24:4-5).**

"Hear me when I call, O God of my righteousness! You have relieved me of my distress; Have mercy on me, and hear my prayer" **(Psalm 4:1).**

_____

_____

_____

_____

_____

_____

_____

_____

_____

_____

_____

_____

_____

Scripture Focus

Read, Meditate, Listen, Pray, Write

"The Lord is my strength and my shield; My heart trusted in Him, and I am helped; Therefore my heart greatly rejoices, And with my song I will praise Him" (Psalm 28:7).

"The Lord has heard my supplication; The Lord will receive my prayer" (Psalm 6:9).

_____

_____

_____

_____

_____

_____

_____

_____

_____

_____

_____

_____

_____

Scripture Focus

Read, Meditate, Listen, Pray, Write

*"Be of good courage, And He shall strengthen your heart, All you who hope in the Lord" (**Psalm 31:24**).*

*"Hear a just cause, O Lord, Attend to my cry; Give ear to my prayer which is not from deceitful lips" (**Psalm 17:1**).*

_____

_____

_____

_____

_____

_____

_____

_____

_____

_____

_____

_____

_____

Scripture Focus

Read, Meditate, Listen, Pray, Write

"For our heart shall rejoice in Him, Because we have trusted in His holy name" (*Psalm 33:21*).

*"Hear my prayer, O Lord, And give ear to my cry, Do not be silent at my tears; For I am a stranger with You, A sojourner, as all my fathers were" (**Psalm 39:12**).*

_____

_____

_____

_____

_____

_____

_____

_____

_____

_____

_____

_____

Scripture Focus

Read, Meditate, Listen, Pray, Write

"The Lord is near to those who have a broken heart, And saves such as have a contrite spirit" **(Psalm 34:18).**

"The Lord will command His lovingkindness in the daytime. And in the night His song shall be with me A prayer to the God of my life" **(Psalm 42:8).**

_____

_____

_____

_____

_____

_____

_____

_____

_____

_____

_____

_____

_____

_____

Scripture Focus

Read, Meditate, Listen, Pray, Write

*"Delight yourself also in the Lord, and He shall give you the desires of your heart" (**Psalm 37:4**).*

*"Hear my prayer, O God; Give ear to the words of my mouth" (**Psalm 54:2**).*

_____

_____

_____

_____

_____

_____

_____

_____

_____

_____

_____

_____

_____

_____

_____

Scripture Focus

Read, Meditate, Listen, Pray, Write

"Would not God search this out? For He knows the secrets of the heart" (**Psalm 44:21**).

"Give ear to my prayer, O God, And do not hide Yourself from my supplication" **Psalm 55:1**

_____

_____

_____

_____

_____

_____

_____

_____

_____

_____

_____

_____

_____

_____

Scripture Focus

Read, Meditate, Listen, Pray, Write

"My mouth shall speak wisdom, and the meditation of my heart shall speak understanding" (**Psalm 49:3**).

"Hear my cry, O God; Attend to my prayer" (**Psalm 61:1**).

_____

_____

_____

_____

_____

_____

_____

_____

_____

_____

_____

_____

_____

_____

Scripture Focus

Read, Meditate, Listen, Pray, Write

"Create in me a clean heart, O God, And renew a steadfast spirit within me" **(Psalm 51:10).**

"O You who hear prayer To You all flesh will come" **(Psalm 65:2).**

_____

_____

_____

_____

_____

_____

_____

_____

_____

_____

_____

_____

_____

_____

Scripture Focus

Read, Meditate, Listen, Pray, Write

"The sacrifices of God are a broken spirit, A broken and a contrite heart These, O God you will not despise" (**Psalms 51:17**).

"But certainly, God has heard me; He has attended to the voice of my prayer" (**Psalms 66:19**).

_____

_____

_____

_____

_____

_____

_____

_____

_____

_____

_____

_____

_____

Scripture Focus

Read, Meditate, Listen, Pray, Write

"Trust in Him at all times, you people, Pour out your heart before Him; God is a refuge for us. Selah" (**Psalm 62:8**).

"Blessed be God, Who has not turned away my prayer, Nor His mercy from me"! (**Psalm 66:20**).

_____

_____

_____

_____

_____

_____

_____

_____

_____

_____

_____

_____

_____

_____

Scripture Focus

Read, Meditate, Listen, Pray, Write

*"If I regard iniquity in my heart, you will not heart, the Lord will not hear me:" (**Psalm 66:18**).*

*"But as for me, my prayer is to You, O Lord in the acceptable time; O God, in the multitude of Your mercy, Hear me in the truth of your salvation" (**Psalm 69:13**).*

_____

_____

_____

_____

_____

_____

_____

_____

_____

_____

_____

_____

_____

_____

Scripture Focus

Read, Meditate, Listen, Pray, Write

"The humble shall see this and be glad; And you who seek God, your hearts shall live" (**Psalm 69:32**).

"O Lord God of host, hear my prayer; Give ear, O God of Jacob! Selah" (**Psalm 84:8**).

Scripture Focus

Read, Meditate, Listen, Pray, Write

"Praise the Lord! I will praise the Lord with my whole heart, In the assembly of the upright and in the congregation" **(Psalm 111:1).**

"Give ear, O Lord, to my prayer; And attend to the voice of my supplications" **(Psalm 86:6).**

_____

_____

_____

_____

_____

_____

_____

_____

_____

_____

_____

_____

Scripture Focus

Read, Meditate, Listen, Pray, Write

"Let my heart be blameless regarding Your statues, That I may not be ashamed" (*Psalm 119:80*).

"Hear my prayer, O Lord, And let my cry come to You" (*Psalm 102:1*).

_____

_____

_____

_____

_____

_____

_____

_____

_____

_____

_____

_____

_____

_____

Scripture Focus

Read, Meditate, Listen, Pray, Write

"A sound heart is life to the body, But envy is rottenness to the bones" (**Proverbs 14:30**).

"He shall regard the prayer of the destitute, And shall not despise their prayer" (**Psalm 102:17**).

_____

_____

_____

_____

_____

_____

_____

_____

_____

_____

_____

_____

_____

Scripture Focus

Read, Meditate, Listen, Pray, Write

"Do not let your heart envy sinners, But be zealous for the fear of the Lord all the day; 18 For surely there is a hereafter, And your hope will not be cut off" (**Proverbs 23:17-18**).

"In return for my love they are my accusers, But I give myself to prayer" (**Psalm 109:4**).

_____

_____

_____

_____

_____

_____

_____

_____

_____

_____

_____

_____

_____

_____

Faith

T*he word Faith is (Pistis) in the Greek and means* conviction, confidence, trust, belief, reliance, trustworthiness, and persuasion.

In the New Testament, faith is the divinely implanted principle of inward confidence, assurance, trust, and reliance in God and all that He says.

*"So then faith comes by hearing and hearing by the Word of God" (**Romans 10:17**).*

We must worship God from a pure heart with complete sincerity of purpose. When our worship is based on the assurance of the justifying power of the blood of Christ, it ushers us into the throne room and the presence of the Almighty God.

Our heart is one of the body's physical organs, the center of one's personality, the seat of one's entire mental and moral activity, containing both rational and emotional elements. It is the seat of feelings, desires, joy, pain, and love. Our heart is also the center for thought understanding and will.

The human heart is the dwelling place of the Lord and Holy Spirit. The omniscient Lord sees into the innermost being where all decisions concerning Him are made. If you are going to prevail in prayer, you must have a forgiving heart.

The heart of an Intercessor should be full of:

Forgiveness	Love	Devotion
Hope	Joy	Serenity
Compassion	Peace	Goodwill
Grace	Longsuffering	Obedience
Mercy	Kindness	Contentment
Delight	Goodness	Cheerfulness
Benevolence	Faithfulness	Giving
Humility	Gentleness	Honesty
Generosity	Self-Control	Sincerity
Liberality	Virtue	Commitment

Scripture Focus

Read, Meditate, Listen, Pray, Write

"Behold the proud, His soul is not upright in him; But the just shall live by his faith" **(Habakkuk 2:4).**

"Let my prayer be set before You as incense, The lifting up of my hands as the evening sacrifice" **(Psalm 141:2).**

_____

_____

_____

_____

_____

_____

_____

_____

_____

_____

_____

_____

_____

_____

Scripture Focus

Read, Meditate, Listen, Pray, Write

"So Jesus answered and said to them, Assuredly, I say to you, if you have faith and do not doubt, you will not only do what was done to this fig tree, but also if you say to this mountain, Be removed and be cast into the sea, it will be done." And whatever things you ask in prayer, believing, you will receive them" **(Matthew 21:21-22).**

"The sacrifice of the wicked is an abomination to the Lord, But the prayer of the upright is His delight" **(Proverbs 15:8).**

_____

_____

_____

_____

_____

_____

_____

_____

_____

_____

_____

Scripture Focus

Read, Meditate, Listen, Pray, Write

*"Do not let your heart envy sinners, But be zealous for the fear of the Lord all the day; For surely there is a hereafter, And your hope will not be cut off." (**Proverbs 23:17-18**).*

*"In return for my love they are my accusers, But I give myself to prayer" (**Psalm 109:4**).*

_____

_____

_____

_____

_____

_____

_____

_____

_____

_____

_____

_____

_____

Scripture Focus

Read, Meditate, Listen, Pray, Write

*"And He said to her, "Daughter be of good cheer; your faith has made you well. Go in peace" (**Luke 8:48**).*

*"Go and tell Hezekiah Thus says the Lord, the God of David your father: "I have heard your prayer, I have seen your tears: surely I will add to your days fifteen years," (**Isaiah 38:5**).*

_____

_____

_____

_____

_____

_____

_____

_____

_____

_____

_____

_____

_____

Scripture Focus

Read, Meditate, Listen, Pray, Write

"For I am not ashamed of the gospel of Christ, for it is the power of God to salvation for everyone who believes, for the Jew first and also for the Greek. For in it the righteousness of God is revealed from faith to faith; as it is written, The just shall live by faith" (**Romans 1:16-17**).

"Even them I will bring to my holy mountain, And make them joyful in My house of prayer. Their burnt offerings and their sacrifices Will be accepted on My altar; For My house shall be called a house of prayer for all nations" (**Isaiah 56:7**).

_____

_____

_____

_____

_____

_____

_____

_____

_____

_____

_____

_____

Scripture Focus

Read, Meditate, Listen, Pray, Write

"Whom God set forth as a propitiation by His blood, through faith, to demonstrate His righteousness, because in His forbearance God had passed over the sins that were previously committed" (**Romans 3:25**).

"Then I set my face toward the Lord God to make request by prayer and supplications, with fasting, sackcloth, and ashes" (**Daniel 9:3**).

_____

_____

_____

_____

_____

_____

_____

_____

_____

_____

_____

Scripture Focus

Read, Meditate, Listen, Pray, Write

"He did not waver at the promise of God through unbelief, but was strengthened in faith, giving glory to God, 21 and being fully convinced that what He had promised He was able to perform" (**Romans 4:20-21**).

"Yes, while I was speaking in prayer, the man Gabriel, whom I had seen in the vision at the beginning, being caused to fly swiftly, reached me about at the time of the evening offering" (**Daniel 9:21**).

_____

_____

_____

_____

_____

_____

_____

_____

_____

_____

_____

_____

71

Scripture Focus

Read, Meditate, Listen, Pray, Write

"Therefore, having been justified by faith, we have peace with God through our Lord Jesus Christ, through whom also we have access by faith into this grace in which we stand, and rejoice in hope of the glory of God" (**Romans 5:1-2**).

"When my soul fainted within me, I remembered the Lord; And my prayer went up to You into Your holy temple" (**Jonah 2:7**).

_____

_____

_____

_____

_____

_____

_____

_____

_____

_____

_____

_____

_____

Scripture Focus

Read, Meditate, Listen, Pray, Write

"So then faith comes by hearing and hearing, by the word of God" **(Romans 10:17).**

"However, this kind does not go out except by prayer and fasting" **(Matthew 17:21).**

_____

_____

_____

_____

_____

_____

_____

_____

_____

_____

_____

_____

_____

_____

Scripture Focus

Read, Meditate, Listen, Pray, Write

"For I say, through the grace given to me, to everyone who is among you, not to think of himself more highly than he ought to think, but to think soberly, as God has dealt to each a measure of faith" (**Romans 12:3**).

"And whatever things you ask in prayer, believing, you will receive" (**Matthew 21:22**).

_____

_____

_____

_____

_____

_____

_____

_____

_____

_____

_____

_____

Scripture Focus

Read, Meditate, Listen, Pray, Write

"Watch, stand fast in the faith, be brave, be strong" (**1 Corinthians 16:13**).

"So He said to them, This kind can come out by nothing but prayer and fasting" (**Mark 9:29**).

_____

_____

_____

_____

_____

_____

_____

_____

_____

_____

_____

_____

_____

_____

Scripture Focus

Read, Meditate, Listen, Pray, Write

*"For we walk by faith, not by sight" (**2 Corinthians 5:7**).*

*"But the angel said to him, "Do not be afraid, Zacharias, for your prayer is heard; and your wife Elizabeth will bear you a son, and you shall call his." (**Luke 1:13**).*

Scripture Focus

Read, Meditate, Listen, Pray, Write

*"Jesus Christ, even we have believed in Christ Jesus, that we might be justified by faith in Christ and not by the works of the law; for by the works of the law no flesh shall be justified" (**Galatians 2:16**).*

*"These all continued with one accord in prayer and supplication, with the women and Mary the mother of Jesus, and with His brothers" (**Acts 1:14**).*

_____

_____

_____

_____

_____

_____

_____

_____

_____

_____

_____

_____

Scripture Focus

Read, Meditate, Listen, Pray, Write

"I have been crucified with Christ; it is no longer I who live, but Christ lives in me; and the life which I now live in the flesh I live by faith in the Son of God who loved me and gave Himself for me" (**Galatians 2:20**).

"But we will give ourselves continually to prayer and to the ministry of the word" (**Acts 6:4**).

_____

_____

_____

_____

_____

_____

_____

_____

_____

_____

_____

_____

Scripture Focus

Read, Meditate, Listen, Pray, Write

"*There is one body, and one Spirit even as we are called in one hope of your calling; One Lord, one faith, one baptism, One God and Father of all who is above all, and through all and in you all*" (**Ephesians 4:4-6**).
[10]

"*Peter was therefore kept in prison, but constant prayer was offered to God for him by the church*" (**Acts 12:5**).

_____

_____

_____

_____

_____

_____

_____

_____

_____

_____

_____

_____

Scripture Focus

Read, Meditate, Listen, Pray, Write

"Peace to the brethren, and love with faith, from God the Father and the Lord Jesus Christ" (**Ephesians 6:23**).

"Brethren, my heart's desire and prayer to God for Israel is that they may be saved" (**Romans 10:1**).

_____

_____

_____

_____

_____

_____

_____

_____

_____

_____

_____

_____

_____

Scripture Focus

Read, Meditate, Listen, Pray, Write

"Only let your conduct be worthy of the gospel of Christ, so that whether I come and see you or am absent, I may hear of your affairs, that you stand fast hear of your affairs, that you stand fast in one spirit, with one mind striving together for the faith of the gospel, 28 and not by any way terrified by your adversaries, which is to them a proof of perdition, but to you of salvation, and that from God" (**Philippians 1:27-28**).

"Rejoicing in hope, patient in tribulation, continuing steadfastly in prayer;" (**Romans 12:12**).

_____

_____

_____

_____

_____

_____

_____

_____

_____

_____

_____

Scripture Focus

Read, Meditate, Listen, Pray, Write

"Rooted and built up in Him and established in the faith, as you have been taught, abounding in it with thanksgiving" (**Colossians 2:7**).

"You also helping together in prayer for us, that thanks may be given by many persons on our behalf for the gift granted to us through many" (**2 Corinthians 1:11**).

_____

_____

_____

_____

_____

_____

_____

_____

_____

_____

_____

_____

_____

Scripture Focus

Read, Meditate, Listen, Pray, Write

"But let us who are of the day be sober, putting on the breastplate of faith and love, and as a helmet the hope of salvation" (1 Thessalonians 5:8).

"Praying always with all prayer and supplication in the Spirit, being watchful to this end with all perseverance and supplication for all the saints" (Ephesians 6:18).

_____

_____

_____

_____

_____

_____

_____

_____

_____

_____

_____

_____

Scripture Focus

Read, Meditate, Listen, Pray, Write

"We are bound to thank God always for you, brethren, as it is fitting, because your faith grows exceedingly, and the love of every one of you all abounds toward each other," **(2 Thessalonians 1:3)**

"Always in every prayer of mine making request for you all with joy," **(Philippians 1:4).**

_____

_____

_____

_____

_____

_____

_____

_____

_____

_____

_____

_____

_____

Scripture Focus

Read, Meditate, Listen, Pray, Write

"So that we ourselves boast of you among the churches of God for your patience and faith in all your persecutions and tribulations you endure" (**2 Thessalonians 1:4**).

"For I know that this will turn out for my deliverance through your prayer and the supply of the Spirit of Jesus Christ," (**Philippians 1:19**).

_____

_____

_____

_____

_____

_____

_____

_____

_____

_____

_____

_____

_____

Scripture Focus

Read, Meditate, Listen, Pray, Write

"Therefore we also pray always for you that our God would count you worthy *of this calling, and fulfill all the good pleasure of His goodness and the work of faith with power" (2 Thessalonians 1:11).*

"Be anxious for nothing, but in everything, by prayer and supplication with thanksgiving, let your request be made known to God" (Philippians 4:6).

Scripture Focus

Read, Meditate, Listen, Pray, Write

"Nor give heed to fables and endless genealogies which cause disputes rather than godly edification which is in faith" (**1 Timothy 1:4**).

"Continue earnestly in prayer, being vigilant in it with thanksgiving;" (**Colossians 4:2**).

_____

_____

_____

_____

_____

_____

_____

_____

_____

_____

_____

_____

_____

_____

"Scripture Focus

Read, Meditate, Listen, Pray, Write

If you instruct the brethren in these things, you will be a good minister of Jesus Christ, nourished in the words of faith and of the good doctrine which you have carefully followed" **(1 Timothy 4:6)**.

"Confess your trespasses to one another, and pray for one another, that you may be healed. The effective, fervent prayer of a righteous man avails much" **(James 5:16)**.

_____

_____

_____

_____

_____

_____

_____

_____

_____

_____

_____

Scripture Focus

Read, Meditate, Listen, Pray, Write

"Let no one despise your youth, but be an example to the believers in word, in conduct, in love, in spirit, in faith, in purity" **(1 Timothy 4:12).**

"And they continued steadfastly in the apostles' doctrine and fellowship, in the breaking of bread, and in prayer" **(Acts 2:42).**

_____

_____

_____

_____

_____

_____

_____

_____

_____

_____

_____

_____

_____

_____

"Scripture Focus

Read, Meditate, Listen, Pray, Write

*But you, O man of God, flee these things and pursue righteousness, godliness, faith, love, patience, gentleness" (**1 Timothy 6:11**).*

*"Therefore I exhort first of all that supplications, prayers, intercessions and giving of thanks be made for all men" (**1 Timothy 2:1**).*

_____

_____

_____

_____

_____

_____

_____

_____

_____

_____

_____

_____

_____

_____

Scripture Focus

Read, Meditate, Listen, Pray, Write

*"Fight the good fight of faith, lay hold on eternal life, to which you were also called and have confessed the good confession in the presence of many witnesses" (**1 Timothy 6:12**).*

*"I thank my God, making mention of you always in my prayers, hearing of your love and faith which you have toward the Lord Jesus and toward all the saints, that the sharing of your faith may become effective by the acknowledgment of every good thing which is in you in Christ Jesus" (**Philemon 1:4-6**).*

_____

_____

_____

_____

_____

_____

_____

_____

_____

_____

_____

91

Scripture Focus

Read, Meditate, Listen, Pray, Write

"And that from childhood you have known the Holy Scriptures, which are able to make you wise for salvation through faith which is in Christ Jesus" (2 Timothy 3:15).

"Who in the days of His flesh, when He had offered up prayers and supplications, with vehement cries and tears to Him who was able to save Him from death, and was heard because of His godly fear" (Hebrews 5:7)

_____

_____

_____

_____

_____

_____

_____

_____

_____

_____

_____

_____

Scripture Focus

Read, Meditate, Listen, Pray, Write

"I have fought the good fight, I have finished the race, I have kept the faith" *(2 Timothy 4:7).*

"Husbands, likewise, dwell with them with understanding, giving honor to the wife, as to the weaker vessel, and as being heirs together of the grace of life, that your prayers may not be hindered" *(1 Peter 3:7).*

_____

_____

_____

_____

_____

_____

_____

_____

_____

_____

_____

_____

Scripture Focus

Read, Meditate, Listen, Pray, Write

"By faith we understand that the worlds were framed by the word of God, so that the things which are seen were not made of things which are visible" (Hebrews 11:3).

"For the eyes of the Lord are on the righteous, And His ears are open to their prayers; But the face of the Lord is against those that do evil." (1 Peter 3:12).

_____

_____

_____

_____

_____

_____

_____

_____

_____

_____

_____

_____

Scripture Focus

Read, Meditate, Listen, Pray, Write

"But without faith it is impossible to please Him, for he who comes to God must believe that He is and that He is a rewarder of those that diligently seek Him" (**Hebrews 11:6**).

"Now when He had taken the scroll, the four living creatures and the twenty-four elders fell down before the Lamb, each having a harp, and golden bowls full of incense, which are the prayers of the saints" (**Revelation 5:8**).

_____

_____

_____

_____

_____

_____

_____

_____

_____

_____

_____

_____

Scripture Focus

Read, Meditate, Listen, Pray, Write

"By faith they passed through the Red Sea as by dry land, whereas The Egyptians, attempting to do so, were drowned" (**Hebrews 11:29**).

"And it happened, as she continued praying before the Lord, that Eli watched her mouth" (**1 Samuel 1:12**).

_____

_____

_____

_____

_____

_____

_____

_____

_____

_____

_____

_____

_____

_____

Scripture Focus

Read, Meditate, Listen, Pray, Write

"By faith the walls of Jericho fell down after they were encircled for seven days" (**Hebrews 11:30**).

"And so it was, when Solomon had finished praying all this prayer and supplication to the Lord, that he arose from before the altar of the Lord, from kneeling on his knees with his hands spread up to heaven" (**1 Kings 8:54**).

_____

_____

_____

_____

_____

_____

_____

_____

_____

_____

_____

_____

Scripture Focus

Read, Meditate, Listen, Pray, Write

"Looking unto Jesus, the author and the finisher of our faith, who for the joy that was set before Him endured the cross, despising the shame, and has sat down at the right hand of the throne of God" (**Hebrews 12:2**).

"When all the people were baptized, it came to pass that Jesus also was baptized; and while He prayed, the heaven was opened" (**Luke 3:21**).

"Knowing that the testing of your faith produces patience" (**James 1:3**).

"But you, beloved building yourselves up on your most holy faith praying in the Holy Spirit "(**Jude 1:20**).

Scripture Focus

Read, Meditate, Listen, Pray, Write

"That the genuineness of your faith, being, much more precious than gold that perishes, though it is tested by fire, may be found to praise, honor and glory at the revelation of Jesus Christ" (**1 Peter 1:7**).

"But you, beloved, building yourselves up in your most holy faith praying in the Holy Spirit" (**Jude 1:20**).

_____

_____

_____

_____

_____

_____

_____

_____

_____

_____

_____

_____

_____

_____

Hope

H ope, is a confident expectation based on concrete certainty. Biblical hope rests on God's promises, particularly those concerning Christ's return. Hope is never inferior to faith but is an extension of faith. Faith is the present possession of grace; hope is confidence in grace's future accomplishment.

> *"Remembering without ceasing your faith, labor of love, and patience of hope in our Lord Jesus Christ in the sight of our God and Father, knowing, beloved brethren, your election by God" (1 Thessalonians 1:3-4).*

> *"Now may the God of hope fill you with all joy and peace in believing, that you may abound in hope by the power of the Holy Spirit" (Romans 15:13).*

Scripture Focus

Read, Meditate, Listen, Pray, Write

"Be of good courage, And He shall strengthen your heart, All you who hope in the Lord" (**Psalm 31:24**)

"Now the birth of Jesus Christ was as follows: After His mother Mary was betrothed to Joseph, before they came together, she was found with child of the Holy Spirit" (**Matthew 1:18).**

_____

_____

_____

_____

_____

_____

_____

_____

_____

_____

_____

_____

_____

_____

Scripture Focus

Read, Meditate, Listen, Pray, Write

"Behold, the eye of the Lord is on those who fear Him On those who hope in His mercy, To deliver their soul from death, And to keep them alive in famine" **(Psalm 33:18-19).**

"I indeed baptize you with water unto repentance, but He who is coming after me is mightier than I, whose sandals I am not worthy to carry. He will baptize you with the Holy Spirit and fire" **(Matthew 3:11).**

_____

_____

_____

_____

_____

_____

_____

_____

_____

_____

_____

_____

Scripture Focus

Read, Meditate, Listen, Pray, Write

"Let Your mercy, O Lord, be upon us, Just as we hope in You (**Psalm 33:22**).

"Go therefore and make disciples of all the nations baptizing them in the name of the Father and of the Son and of the Holy Spirit" (**Matthew 28:19**).

_____

_____

_____

_____

_____

_____

_____

_____

_____

_____

_____

_____

Scripture Focus

Read, Meditate, Listen, Pray, Write

"For in You, O Lord, I hope; You will hear, O Lord my God" (**Psalm 38:15**)

"For he will be great in the sight of the Lord, and shall drink neither wine nor strong drink. He will also be filled with the Holy Spirit, even from His mother's womb" (**Luke 1:15**).

_____

_____

_____

_____

_____

_____

_____

_____

_____

_____

_____

_____

_____

_____

Scripture Focus

Read, Meditate, Listen, Pray, Write

"Why are you cast down, O my soul? And why are you disquieted within me? Hope in God, for I shall yet praise Him For the help of His countenance" **(Psalm 42:5).**

"And the angel answered and said to her, The Holy Spirit will come upon you, and the power of the Highest will overshadow you, therefore, also, that Holy One who is to be born will be called the Son of God." **(Luke 1:35).**

_____

_____

_____

_____

_____

_____

_____

_____

_____

_____

_____

_____

Scripture Focus

Read, Meditate, Listen, Pray, Write

"For you are my hope, O Lord God; You are my trust from my youth"
(Psalm 71:5).

*"And it happened, when Elizabeth heard the greeting of Mary, that the babe leaped in her womb; and Elizabeth was filled with the Holy Spirit" **(Luke 1:41).***

_____

_____

_____

_____

_____

_____

_____

_____

_____

_____

_____

_____

_____

Scripture Focus

Read, Meditate, Listen, Pray, Write

"But I will hope continually, And will praise You yet more and more" **(Psalm 71:14).**

"And the Holy Spirit descended in bodily form like a dove upon Him, and a voice came from heaven which said, You are My beloved Son; in You I am well pleased" **(Luke 3:22).**

_____

_____

_____

_____

_____

_____

_____

_____

_____

_____

_____

_____

_____

Scripture Focus

Read, Meditate, Listen, Pray, Write

"You are my hiding place and my shield; I hope in your word" (**Psalm 119:114**).

"Then Jesus being filled with the Holy Spirit, returned from the Jordan and was led by the Spirit into the wilderness" (**Luke 4:1**).

_____

_____

_____

_____

_____

_____

_____

_____

_____

_____

_____

_____

_____

Scripture Focus

Read, Meditate, Listen, Pray, Write

*"Uphold me according to Your word, that I may live; And do not let me be ashamed of my hope (**Psalm 119:116**).*

*"For the Holy Spirit will teach you in that very hour what you ought to say" (**Luke 12:12**)*

_____

_____

_____

_____

_____

_____

_____

_____

_____

_____

_____

_____

_____

Scripture Focus

Read, Meditate, Listen, Pray, Write

"I wait for the Lord, my soul waits, And in His word I do hope" (**Psalm 130:5**).

"I did not know Him, but He who sent me to baptize with water said to me, Upon whom you see the Spirit descending, and remaining on Him, this is He who baptizes with the Holy Spirit" (**John 1:33**).

_____

_____

_____

_____

_____

_____

_____

_____

_____

_____

_____

_____

Scripture Focus

Read, Meditate, Listen, Pray, Write

"Happy is he who has the God of Jacob for his help, Whose hope is in the Lord his God" (**Psalm 146:5**).

"But the Helper, the Holy Spirit, whom the Father will send in My name, He will teach you all things, and bring to your remembrance all things that I said to you" (**John 14:26**).

_____

_____

_____

_____

_____

_____

_____

_____

_____

_____

_____

_____

_____

Scripture Focus

Read, Meditate, Listen, Pray, Write

"The hope of the righteous will be gladness, But the expectation of the wicked will perish" **(Proverbs 10:28).**

"And when He had said this, He breathed on them, and said to them, "Receive the Holy Spirit" **(John 20:22).**

_____

_____

_____

_____

_____

_____

_____

_____

_____

_____

_____

_____

_____

THE HEART OF AN INTERCESSOR

Scripture Focus

Read, Meditate, Listen, Pray, Write

"Hope deferred makes the heart sick, But when the desire comes, it is a tree of life" (**Proverbs 13:12**).

"But you shall receive power when the Holy Spirit has come upon you; and you shall be witnesses to Me in Jerusalem, and in all Judea and Samaria and to the end of the earth" (**Acts 1:8**).

_____

_____

_____

_____

_____

_____

_____

_____

_____

_____

_____

_____

_____

Scripture Focus

Read, Meditate, Listen, Pray, Write

"Blessed is the man who trusts in the Lord, And whose hope is the Lord" (**Jeremiah 17:7**).

"And they were all filled with the Holy Spirit and began to speak with other tongues, as the Spirit gave them utterance" (**Acts 1:4**).

_____

_____

_____

_____

_____

_____

_____

_____

_____

_____

_____

_____

_____

_____

Scripture Focus

Read, Meditate, Listen, Pray, Write

"Now hope does not disappoint, because the love of God has been poured out in our hearts by the Holy Spirit who was given to us" **(Romans 5:5).**

*"Therefore being exalted to the right hand of God, and having received from the Father the promise of the Holy Spirit, He poured out this which you now see and hear" **(Acts 2:33).***

_____

_____

_____

_____

_____

_____

_____

_____

_____

_____

_____

Scripture Focus

Read, Meditate, Listen, Pray, Write

"Rejoicing in hope, patient in tribulation, continuing steadfastly in prayer"
(Romans 12:12).

*"Then Peter said to them, Repent, and let every one of you be baptized in the name of Jesus Christ for the remission of sins; and you shall receive the gift of the Holy Spirit" (**Acts 2:38).**

_____

_____

_____

_____

_____

_____

_____

_____

_____

_____

_____

_____

Scripture Focus

Read, Meditate, Listen, Pray, Write

*"For whatever things were written before were written for our learning, that we through the patience and comfort of the Scriptures might have hope" (**Romans 15:4**)*

*"Then the churches throughout all Judea, Galilee, and Samaria had peace and were edified. And walking in the fear of the Lord and in the comfort of the Holy Spirit, they were multiplied" (**Acts 9:31**).*

Scripture Focus

Read, Meditate, Listen, Pray, Write

"Now may the God of hope fill you with all joy and peace in believing that you may abound in hope by the power of the Holy Spirit" (**Romans 15:13**).

"How God anointed Jesus of Nazareth with the Holy Spirit and with power, who went about doing good and healing all who oppressed by the devil, for God was with Him" (**Acts 10:38**).

_____

_____

_____

_____

_____

_____

_____

_____

_____

_____

_____

_____

_____

119

Scripture Focus

Read, Meditate, Listen, Pray, Write

"And our hope for you is steadfast, because we know that as you are partakers of the sufferings, so also you will partake of the consolation" (**2 Corinthians 1:7**).

"And as I began to speak, the Holy Spirit fell upon them, as upon us at the beginning" (**Acts 11:15**).

_____

_____

_____

_____

_____

_____

_____

_____

_____

_____

_____

_____

_____

Scripture Focus

Read, Meditate, Listen, Pray, Write

"Not boasting of things beyond measure, that is, in other men's labor, but having hope, that is your faith is increased, we shall be greatly enlarged by you in our sphere" (**2 Corinthians 10:15**).

"And the disciples were filled with joy and with the Holy Spirit" (**Acts 13:52**).

_____

_____

_____

_____

_____

_____

_____

_____

_____

_____

_____

_____

Scripture Focus

Read, Meditate, Listen, Pray, Write

*"For we through the Spirit eagerly wait for the hope of righteousness by faith" (**Galatians 5:5**).*

*"So God, who knows the heart, acknowledge them by giving them the Holy Spirit, just as He did to us, and made no distinction between us and them, purifying their hearts by faith" (**Acts 15:8**).*

_____

_____

_____

_____

_____

_____

_____

_____

_____

_____

_____

_____

_____

Scripture Focus

Read, Meditate, Listen, Pray, Write

"The eyes of your understanding being enlightened; that you may know what is the hope of His calling, what are the riches of the glory of His inheritance in the saints, and what is the exceeding greatness of His power toward us who believe, according to the working of His mighty power" (*Ephesians 1:18-19*).

"And when Paul had laid hands on them, the Holy Spirit came upon them, and they spoke with tongues and prophesied" (*Acts 19:6*).

_____

_____

_____

_____

_____

_____

_____

_____

_____

_____

_____

Scripture Focus

Read, Meditate, Listen, Pray, Write

"There is one body and one Spirit, just as you were called in one hope of your calling; one Lord, one faith, one baptism; 6 one God and Father of all, is above all, and through all and in you all" (**Ephesians 4:4**).

"Therefore take heed to yourselves and to all the flock, among which the Holy Spirit has made you overseers, to shepherd the church of God which He purchased with His own blood" (Acts 20:28).

_____

_____

_____

_____

_____

_____

_____

_____

_____

_____

_____

_____

Scripture Focus

Read, Meditate, Listen, Pray, Write

"According to my earnest expectation and hope that in nothing I shall be ashamed, but with all boldness, as always, so now also Christ will be magnified in my body, whether by life or by death" (**Philippians 1:20**).

"For the kingdom of God is not eating and drinking, but righteousness and peace and joy in the Holy Spirit" (**Romans 14:17**).

_____

_____

_____

_____

_____

_____

_____

_____

_____

_____

_____

_____

Scripture Focus

Read, Meditate, Listen, Pray, Write

"To them God willed to make known what are the riches of the glory of this mystery among the Gentiles: which is Christ in you, the hope of glory" **(Colossians 1:27).**

"Now may the God of hope fill you with all joy and peace in believing, that you may abound in hope by the power of the Holy Spirit" **(Romans 15:13).**

_____

_____

_____

_____

_____

_____

_____

_____

_____

_____

_____

_____

Scripture Focus

Read, Meditate, Listen, Pray, Write

"But let us who are of the day be sober, putting on the breastplate of faith and love, and as a helmet the hope of salvation" (**1 Thessalonians 5:8**).

"These things we also speak, not in words which man's wisdom teaches but which the Holy Spirit teaches, comparing spiritual things with spiritual" (**1 Corinthians 2:13**).

_____

_____

_____

_____

_____

_____

_____

_____

_____

_____

_____

_____

Scripture Focus

Read, Meditate, Listen, Pray, Write

*"Therefore gird up the loins of your mind, be sober, and rest your hope fully upon the grace that is to be brought to you at the revelation of Jesus Christ;" (**1 Peter 1:13**).*

*"Or do you not know that your body is the temple of the Holy Spirit who is in you, whom you have from God, and you are not your own? 20 For you were bought at a price; therefore glorify God in your body and in your spirit, which are God's" (**1 Corinthians 6:19-20**).*

_____

_____

_____

_____

_____

_____

_____

_____

_____

_____

_____

Scripture Focus

Read, Meditate, Listen, Pray, Write

*"He indeed was foreordained before the foundation of the world, but was manifest in these last times for you who through Him believe in God, who raised Him from the dead and gave Him glory so that your faith and hope are in God" (**1 Peter 1:20-21**).*

*"In Him you also trusted, after you heard the word of truth the gospel of your salvation; in whom also, having believed, you were sealed with the Holy Spirit of promise" (**Ephesians 1:13**).*

_____

_____

_____

_____

_____

_____

_____

_____

_____

_____

_____

_____

Scripture Focus

Read, Meditate, Listen, Pray, Write

"But sanctify the Lord God in your hearts, and always be ready to give a defense to everyone who asks you a reason for the hope that is in you with meekness and fear" (**1 Peter 3:15**).

"Not by works of righteousness which we have done, but according to His mercy He saved us, through the washing of regeneration and renewing of the Holy Spirit" (**Titus 3:5**).

_____

_____

_____

_____

_____

_____

_____

_____

_____

_____

_____

_____

Scripture Focus

Read, Meditate, Listen, Pray, Write

"And everyone that has this hope in Him purifies himself just as He is pure" (1 John 3:3).

"God also bearing witness both with signs and wonders, with various miracles, and gifts of the Holy Spirit, according to His own will?" (Hebrews 2:4).

_____

_____

_____

_____

_____

_____

_____

_____

_____

_____

_____

_____

_____

Love

Love (agape) - Agape denotes an undefeatable benevolence and unconquerable goodwill that always seeks the highest good of the other person, no matter what he does.

Love is self-giving; it freely gives without asking for anything in return.

Agape is more a love by choice, whereas Phileo is love by chance. Agape engages the will rather than the emotion. Agape describes the unconditional love God has for the world.

The Greatest Gift

"Though I speak with the tongues of men and of angels, but have not love, I have become sounding brass of a clanging cymbal. And though I have the gift of prophesy, and understand all mysteries and all knowledge, and though I have all faith, so that I could remove mountains, but have not love, I am nothing. And though I bestow all my goods to feed the poor, and though I give my body to be burned, but have not love, it profits me nothing. Love suffers long and is kind; love does not envy; love does not parade itself, is not puffed up; does not behave rudely, does not seek its own, is not provoked, thinks no evil; does not rejoice in iniquity, but rejoices in the truth; bears all things, believes all things, hopes all things, endures all things, Love never fails, But whether there are

prophecies, they will fail; whether there are tongues, they will cease; whether there is knowledge, it will vanish away. For we know in part and we prophecy in part. But when that which is perfect has come, then that which is in part will be done away. When I was a child I spoke as a child, I spoke as a child, I understand as a child, I thought as a child; but when I became a man, I put away childish things. For now we see in a mirror dimly, but then face to face. Now I know in part, but then I shall know just also am known. And now abide faith, hope, love, these three; but the greatest of these is love" (1 Corinthians 13:1-13).

Love: The Qualifying Factor

"For God so loved the world that He gave His only begotten Son that whoever believes in Him should not perish but have everlasting life" (John 3:16).

We are blessed beyond measure because of the Agape, unconditional love, of the Almighty God. Agape love is the love the Father desires for us to experience. As you journey through the scriptures of love, may you encounter the benevolence and unconditional love of God.

May God's love, grace, favor, and peace, be upon you as you pray, intercede, and carry the bloodstain banner.

Scripture Focus

Read, Meditate, Listen, Pray, Write

"But let all those rejoice who put their trust in You; Let them ever shout for joy, because You defend them; Let those also who love Your name Be joyful in You" (**Psalm 5:11**).

"Owe no one anything except to love one another for he who loves another has fulfilled the law" (**Romans 13:8**).

_____

_____

_____

_____

_____

_____

_____

_____

_____

_____

_____

_____

_____

_____

Scripture Focus

Read, Meditate, Listen, Pray, Write

"I WILL love You, O Lord, my strength" (**Psalm 18:1**).

"Love does no harm to a neighbor; therefore love is the fulfillment of the law" (**Romans 13:10**).

_____

_____

_____

_____

_____

_____

_____

_____

_____

_____

_____

_____

_____

_____

Scripture Focus

Read, Meditate, Listen, Pray, Write

"Because he has set his love upon Me, therefore I will deliver him; I will set him on high, because he has known My name" (**Psalm 91:14**

"But as it is written: Eye has not seen, nor ear heard, Nor have entered into the heart of man The things which God has prepared for those who love Him" (**1 Corinthians 2:9).**

_____

_____

_____

_____

_____

_____

_____

_____

_____

_____

_____

_____

_____

_____

Scripture Focus

Read, Meditate, Listen, Pray, Write

"You who love the Lord, hate evil! He preserves the souls of His saints; He delivers them out of the hand of the wicked" (**Psalm 97:10**)

"For the love of Christ compels us, because we judge thus: that if One died for all, then all died; 15 and He died for all, that those who live should live no longer for themselves, but for Him who died for them and rose again" (**2 Corinthians 5:14**)

Scripture Focus

Read, Meditate, Listen, Pray, Write

"I LOVE the Lord, because He has heard My voice and my supplications" (**Psalm 116:1**).

"For in Christ Jesus neither circumcision nor uncircumcision avails anything, but faith working through love" (**Galatians 5:6**).

_____

_____

_____

_____

_____

_____

_____

_____

_____

_____

_____

_____

_____

Scripture Focus

Read, Meditate, Listen, Pray, Write

"Look upon me and be merciful to me, As Your custom is toward those who love Your name" (**Psalm 119:132**).

"For you, brethren have been called to liberty; only do not use liberty as an opportunity for the flesh, but through love serve one another" (**Galatians 5:13**).

_____

_____

_____

_____

_____

_____

_____

_____

_____

_____

_____

_____

Scripture Focus

Read, Meditate, Listen, Pray, Write

"Hatred stirs up strife, But love covers all sins" **(Proverbs 10:12).**
"Let brotherly love continue" **(Hebrews 13:1).**

_____

_____

_____

_____

_____

_____

_____

_____

_____

_____

_____

_____

_____

_____

Scripture Focus

Read, Meditate, Listen, Pray, Write

"Many waters cannot quench love, Nor can the floods drown it. If a man would give for love All the wealth of his house, It would be utterly despised" **(Song of Solomon 8:7).**

"Love is a manifestation of growth in God"

Since you have purified your souls in obeying the truth through the Spirit in sincere love of the brethren, love one another fervently with a pure heart.

_____

_____

_____

_____

_____

_____

_____

_____

_____

_____

_____

_____

Scripture Focus

Read, Meditate, Listen, Pray, Write

"The Lord has appeared of old to me, saying: "Yes, I have loved you with an everlasting love; Therefore with lovingkindness I have drawn you" (*Jeremiah 31:3*).

"I drew them with gentle cords, With bands of love, And I was to them as those who take the yoke from their neck. I stooped and fed them" (*Hosea 11:4*).

_____

_____

_____

_____

_____

_____

_____

_____

_____

_____

_____

_____

Scripture Focus

Read, Meditate, Listen, Pray, Write

*"But I say to you, love your enemies, bless those who curse you, do good to those who hate you, and pray for those who spitefully use you and persecute you," (**Matthew 5:44**).*

*"I will heal their backsliding, I will love them freely, For My anger has turned away from him" (**Hosea 14:4**).*

_____

_____

_____

_____

_____

_____

_____

_____

_____

_____

_____

_____

_____

_____

Scripture Focus

Read, Meditate, Listen, Pray, Write

"That the genuineness of your faith, being, much more precious than gold that perishes, though it is tested by fire, may be found to praise, honor and glory at the revelation of Jesus Christ" (**1 Peter 1:7**).

"But you, beloved, building yourselves up in your most holy faith praying in the Holy Spirit" (**Jude 1:20**).

_____

_____

_____

_____

_____

_____

_____

_____

_____

_____

_____

_____

_____

_____

Scripture Focus

Read, Meditate, Listen, Pray, Write

*"A new commandment I give to you, that you love one another; as I have loved you, that you also love one another" (**John 13:34**).*

*"And said, My Lord, if I have now found favor in Your sight, do not pass on by Your servant" (**Genesis 18:3**).*

_____

_____

_____

_____

_____

_____

_____

_____

_____

_____

_____

_____

_____

Scripture Focus

Read, Meditate, Listen, Pray, Write

"By this all will know that you are My disciples, if you have love for one another" **(John 13:35).**

"But the Lord was with Joseph and showed him mercy, and he gave him favor in the sight of the keeper of the prison" **(Genesis 39:21).**

_____

_____

_____

_____

_____

_____

_____

_____

_____

_____

_____

_____

_____

_____

Scripture Focus

Read, Meditate, Listen, Pray, Write

*"He who has My commandments and keeps them, it is he who loves Me. And he who loves Me will be loved by My Father, and I will love him and manifest Myself to him' (**John 14:21**).*

*"And the Lord had given the people favor in the sight of the Egyptians, so that they granted them what they requested. Thus they plundered the Egyptians" (**Exodus 12:36**).*

_____

_____

_____

_____

_____

_____

_____

_____

_____

_____

_____

Scripture Focus

Read, Meditate, Listen, Pray, Write

"Jesus answered and said to him if anyone loves Me, he will keep My word; and My Father will love him, and We will come to him and make Our home with him" (**John 14:23**).

"And the child Samuel grew in stature, and in favor both with the Lord and men" (**1 Samuel 2:26**).

_____

_____

_____

_____

_____

_____

_____

_____

_____

_____

_____

_____

_____

Scripture Focus

Read, Meditate, Listen, Pray, Write

"As the Father loved Me, I also have loved you; abide in My love" **(John 15:9).**

"Now when the turn came for Esther the daughter of Abihail the uncle of Mordecai, who had taken her as his daughter, to go into the king, she requested nothing but what Hegai the king's eunuch, the custodian of the women, advised. And Esther obtained favor in the sight of all who saw her" (Esther 2:15).

_____

_____

_____

_____

_____

_____

_____

_____

_____

_____

_____

_____

Scripture Focus

Read, Meditate, Listen, Pray, Write

"If you keep My commandments, you will abide in My love, just as I have kept My Father's commandments and abide in His love" (**John 15:10**).

"You have granted me life and favor, And Your care has preserved my spirit" (**Job 10:12**).

_____

_____

_____

_____

_____

_____

_____

_____

_____

_____

_____

_____

_____

_____

Scripture Focus

Read, Meditate, Listen, Pray, Write

"This is my commandment, that you love one another as I have loved you" (**John 15:12**).

"For You, O Lord, will bless the righteous; With favor you will surround him as with a shield" (**Psalm 5:12**).

_____

_____

_____

_____

_____

_____

_____

_____

_____

_____

_____

_____

_____

Scripture Focus

Read, Meditate, Listen, Pray, Write

"Greater love has no one than this than to lay down one's life for his friends" (**John 15:13**).

"For His anger is but for a moment, His favor is for life; Weeping may endure for a night, But joy comes in the morning" (**Psalm 30:5**).

_____

_____

_____

_____

_____

_____

_____

_____

_____

_____

_____

_____

_____

_____

Scripture Focus

Read, Meditate, Listen, Pray, Write

"Now hope does not disappoint, because the love of God has been poured out in our hearts by the Holy Spirit who was given to us" (**Romans 5:5**).

"For You are the glory of their strength, And in Your favor our horn is exalted" (**Psalm 89:17**).

_____

_____

_____

_____

_____

_____

_____

_____

_____

_____

_____

_____

_____

Scripture Focus

Read, Meditate, Listen, Pray, Write

"But God demonstrate His own love toward us, in that while we were still sinners, Christ died for us" **(Romans 5:8).**

"You will arise and have mercy on Zion; For the time to favor her, Yes, the set time, has come" **(Psalm 102:13).**

_____

_____

_____

_____

_____

_____

_____

_____

_____

_____

_____

_____

_____

_____

Scripture Focus

Read, Meditate, Listen, Pray, Write

"For I am persuaded that neither death nor life, nor angels nor principalities nor powers, nor things present nor things to come, 39 nor height, nor depth, nor any other created thing, shall be able to separate us from the love of God which is in Christ Jesus" (**Romans 8:38-39**).

"And so find favor and high esteem In the sight of God and man" (**Proverbs 3:4**).

_____

_____

_____

_____

_____

_____

_____

_____

_____

_____

_____

Scripture Focus

Read, Meditate, Listen, Pray, Write

"Be kindly affectionate to one another with brotherly love, in honor giving preference to one another" **(Romans 12:10).**

"For whoever finds me finds life, And obtains favor from the Lord;" **(Proverbs 8:35).**

_____

_____

_____

_____

_____

_____

_____

_____

_____

_____

_____

_____

_____

Scripture Focus

Read, Meditate, Listen, Pray, Write

"And walk in love, as Christ also has loved us and given Himself for us, an offering and a sacrifice to God for a sweet-smelling aroma" (**Ephesians 5:2**).

"Good understanding gains favor, But the way of the unfaithful is hard" (**Proverbs 13:15**).

_____

_____

_____

_____

_____

_____

_____

_____

_____

_____

_____

_____

_____

Scripture Focus

Read, Meditate, Listen, Pray, Write

*"For God has not given us a spirit of fear, but of power and of love and of a sound mind" (**2 Timothy 1:7**).*

*"He who finds a wife finds a good thing, And obtains favor from the Lord" (**Proverbs 18:22**).*

_____

_____

_____

_____

_____

_____

_____

_____

_____

_____

_____

_____

_____

Scripture Focus

Read, Meditate, Listen, Pray, Write

"But whoever keeps His word, truly the love of God is perfected in him. By this we know that we are in Him" **(1 John 2:5).**

"Then the angel said to her," Do not be afraid, Mary, for you have found favor with God" **(Luke 1:30).**

_____

_____

_____

_____

_____

_____

_____

_____

_____

_____

_____

_____

_____

Scripture Focus

Read, Meditate, Listen, Pray, Write

"*Behold what manner of love the Father has bestowed on us, that we should be called children of God! Therefore the world does not know us, because it did not know Him*" (**1 John 3:1**).

"*So continuing daily with one accord in the temple, and breaking bread from house to house, they ate their food with gladness and simplicity of heart, praising God and having favor with all the people. And the Lord added to the church daily those who were being saved*" (**Acts 2:46-47**).

_____

_____

_____

_____

_____

_____

_____

_____

_____

_____

_____

_____

Scripture Focus

Read, Meditate, Listen, Pray, Write

"In this the love of God was manifested toward us, that God has sent His only begotten Son into the world, that we might live through Him. 10 In this love, not that we loved God, but that He loved us and sent His Son to be the propitiation for our sins" **(1 John 4:9-10).**

"Therefore He is also able to save to the uttermost those who come to God through Him, since He always lives to make intercession for them" **(Hebrews 7:25).**

_____

_____

_____

_____

_____

_____

_____

_____

_____

_____

_____

_____

ABOUT THE AUTHOR

Jenille Daniels is a wife, mother, and visionary and founder of Designs by Creativity in Los Angeles, California. Called by God as an Intercessor and Prophetic Voice to Pray, Intercede and Proclaim Liberty to her generation and the generations to come. She stands upon the authority of God's Word to see healing and deliverance in the lives of those that are held bound and captive in addiction, hurt, pain, depression, and rejection. By the grace of God, Jenille has been healed and delivered from substance abuse for 21 plus years!

She attended ICDC College and graduated with a diploma in Alcohol and Drug Counseling. She is a member of Open-Door Worship Center Inc, under the leadership of Bishop Deon Douglas and Prophetess Fannette Douglas.

Author, Jenille Daniels, created the Heart of an Intercessor Prophetic Prayer Journal to encourage you to press into hearing God's voice through His Word, Prayer, Praise, Worship, and spending time in His Presence.

In *The Heart of an Intercessor Prophetic Prayer Journal*, you will write it out and face it on the paper. You will Cry out to God, Worship, Praise, and Travail in Prayer. Expect to RECEIVE your MIRACLE when you have released and let go of what has been holding you back! Know that God sees, hears, and knows EVERYTHING concerning you, for He is the revealing one.

Through this Prophetic Prayer Journal, by the Leading of Holy Spirit, you will be taken on a spiritual journey to commune with God the Father through His Son Jesus Christ.

God has a created plan, purpose, and destiny for your life!